Clear Religions

Clear Religions:
A Religion that Accepts All Religions
by Christopher Buteau

2020 by Christopher Buteau

ISBN: 9798693690998

Symbol

I decided if anyone wanted to adopt this, they would want a symbol to identify with. If I did not choose a symbol one would be chosen by someone else.

So the story about this book: It started with *Just Science,* the first book I tried to write for this concept. I was going to try to reboot religion with the scientific method. Texts were intended observations that would be updated regularly.

But soon I found I added commentary. I realized I was still asking people to change teams in religion, and what I really want is for people to let go.

And then I realized what the reboot of religion was. It was this: there is no religion but we steal the stories from all religions. We have Babylonian, Greek, Roman, Egyptian, Indian, Nordish, Chinese and Japanese gods to choose from.

You name it, we steal it, and talk about it almost like it is real, and the religion becomes a bit like storytelling.

I want to try this exercise: Write down a story from your past. Try to remember the details of the scene in question and incorporate some of it into the story. Practice telling the story in groups.

There is no religion.

This is our symbol the zero with the slash.

The font does not matter; the slash does.

(Why? because the guy writing this page likes his slashed zeros that's why.)

Because it is *totally* a zero no chance in being an O. Got that. Good. Moving on.

We help move away from the manipulation of old religions and steal the good parts for ourselves and future generations.

The idea is this:
The doubt of existence will always be the struggle, but no clear byline is the correct answer by any stretch. Accept them all and broaden your pantheon.

Gods reflect our beliefs and development.

Find your strength in YOU and OTHERS.

Always move forward.

Forewords

Too much preamble

It must be said that this has too much before the content
The main content is Declarations, Stories, and Opinions
If you find yourself saying "Boring…." skip ahead.

Whom this book is targeted at.

If you are someone who likes the stories that have a lesson in religion but do not like how people use religion to feel better than others this might be a good book for you.

If you have always found other religions fascinating and wondered why no one else merges these religions into a nonjudgemental religion, this might be a good book for you.

If you think all life is connected (it is) but you don't like mystical mumbo jumbo. This might be a book for you.

If you are a closed-minded individual who thinks that they are all grown up and have nothing new to learn this is NOT a good book for you.

Perhaps this could be a fad in coffee table books, or a book that everyone gifts and no one reads.

But here is the true hope:
If I publish this, warts and all, it may actually spark discussion. Because I really believe that is what the whole human race needs to do. To discuss and attempt to at least see ALL SIDES of the ISSUE.

Maybe not agree but they UNDERSTAND.

I don't like that O.J. killed his ex-wife and her boyfriend.
But I UNDERSTAND why it happened.

Why I published this book.

Many people told me don't bother.
Most people ignored the fact that I kept saying "I think I will publish something..".
Many people told me that what I was trying to write about was too big.
But I just wanted to try to bring something new to the religion or non-religion discussion.

See I myself had been happily non-religious for years. Decades even. And when I was seeing a therapist and they were trying to get a handle on my worldview (there is a word once you learn you never stop using), they said, "Wow it is like you are spiritual but not religious at all."

And I liked that description.

Not targeted at you

Certain stories and declarations may feel like they are directly related to people close to me. They aren't.

This is an exercise of my thoughts.

If some of those thoughts involve things you said or did, good. That means you are worth keeping around.

I am not trying to write something to call you out.

Declarations

First Rule

No violence shall be done in the name of Clear Religions.
If you are doing violence and saying because..
Clear Religions or… Clear Religions made me do it…
You are doing it wrong and should start over.

No more rules besides that ….

You should already understand the basic rules of being a human if you have lived on this planet for any time.

Don't be a dick...seriously it is that simple...

Goals

Note: Most of these goals are stolen from my first concept Just Science.

Clarity

Everything should be written succinctly and understandably.

Review

Everything should be reviewed before going public.

Fact versus Fiction

If text is to exist it should be clear if it is stating facts at the time or opinions.

Fiction can be useful to illustrate a point. Opinions tend to lose their luster as the world changes as it does.

Origins

Every religion has a creation myth for the gods in this world and for the people in this world.

Long ago (close to 14 billion years at the last calculation) the big bang occurred.

Immediately after this, there was a war between matter and antimatter. When they come in contact matter and antimatter will destroy each other and release energy. This is the background energy of the universe cosmologists talk about today. It is not from the big bang but the war between matter and antimatter.

Matter won (strength in numbers is the prevailing theory), and over time matter coalesced, first into protons and electrons, and then eventually hydrogen, the first and simplest atom. This is why out of the elements hydrogen is still the most plentiful; at one point that was all we had.

As time went on gravity gathered hydrogen together enough to become so dense that the first stars ignited. Within the furnaces of these stars many other elements were forged.

These stars, if they ran out of hydrogen, they would fuse helium. Once they ran out of helium they would fuse lithium, and so on, until the stars formed iron. Iron would start to absorb some of the heat of the stellar fusion reactor. The delicate balance of gravity and an explosion that is a star ends, and it would collapse inward and then explode, forming all the other known elements we have come across. This is a supernova.

Many billion years passed before our galaxy and solar system started to form. We know this because the first 4 planets are of a rocky composition whose elements can only come from many, many supernovae.

On the third planet from the sun in our solar system, the conditions were ideal for brewing amino acids. Somehow, someway, life started and continues to evolve until this day.

Within the 14 billion years of the universe the earth has existed for only 5 billion years.
Within that 5 billion years, humans and particularly their societal ways have been around only something like 10,000 years. Within this timeframe, you as an individual, get probably just under 100 years.

Visualize the scale of time from when the universe began (twelve billion years) to stars creating enough elements...to create our solar system for the earth (five billion years) to create life to lead to now (ten thousand for civilization).

Life is short.

Did you know we are all StarDust?

Did you know that, close to fourteen billion years ago, the big bang happened?

There may be a more exact measurement by the time you read this...but just swallow the scope of the time that has passed before you, your family, or even humans, or even primates.
Or even life on earth. Or even earth ...

Over a relatively small amount of time, many Stars came and went.

When stars are smaller, like our sun, they fade out very slowly.
But when they are massive they reach the point they are making iron.

See as a star runs out of hydrogen to fuse into helium, the process keeps going because of momentum and the growing gravity that presses on the center of a star.

The gravity will keep fusing higher and higher up the periodic table until it reaches iron.

And see, iron absorbs the heat energy of a star.

And the tremendous explosion that is fusion, and the tremendous power of gravity that keep a star at bay—lose their continual battle. Gravity crushes everything in a blink of the eye. Actually less time than an eye blink. And then the star explodes and all the other heavier elements on the chart get made in the explosion.

So the next time you look at a periodic chart, think of stars exploding just to make all that.

It is a fact that we are all made of atoms created in the majestical furnaces of the universe called stars.

In fact, the solar system we live in contains 4 rocky planets made of elements that must have taken millions or billions of years to produce, from many different stars.

Each human, each animal, each plant, each building, each ocean is made of molecules made from atoms that were produced in stars and in supernovae.

We are all literally stardust.

So stop saying we ARE NOT SIMILAR.

Computers

As a writer of this text, living in the new millennium, computers are such a large part of life. It is inevitable that they will take over major parts of life.

The current level of computers and software is this: in most middle income households each parent owns a computer that they keep in their pocket.

Computers have progressed from the points of filling large rooms to fitting on desks, and on to fitting in our pockets. The computers in our pockets place voice calls to anywhere on earth, if someone has shared the number with us.

And the Internet has begun—something created to survive the cold war is something sharing information is built on.

If this is being read when no one can remember these days, it makes these statements old and out of touch.

Everything deserves a reboot.

At this period there exists different flavors of executing environments, but the same rules hold true. Is it behaving incorrectly, maybe we should reboot it.

Technology is flawed because it is human.

How often have you executed a bunch of tasks in one day when you realize you forget a specific line item on one of those tasks? A lot of people decide, "Oh I am a fucking idiot", and I am telling you—say "I am fucking human."

You as a human will always make mistakes.

So the original software and hardware of whatever was made to make the stuff you use now was originally influenced by humans.

Accept there will always be flaws in the world, no matter how many iterations.

Also, when it comes to computers, buy what you can afford and you understand.
Being a fan (I just buy Apple, I just buy Google) does not help YOU at all.

Standing on the Shoulders of Giants

It is good when incrementing (moving it forward) technology of any kind to remember humility.

Upon discovering classical physics and then inventing algebra Newton supposedly said he was "standing on the shoulders of giants."

Remember, everything comes from the first stone tool.

I respect that as a constant; I hope others agree.

The Gods we already Know

The following gods are still in our culture.

The planets in the solar system were named after Roman gods. We are using the Roman calendar. This is both a bunch of gods names and certain emperors (July = Julius, August = Augustus). Also the Roman calendar ends with prefixes that represent 7, 8, 9, 10 (September, October, November, December) at the points 9, 10, 11, 12 this is because the original calendar was only 10 months long.

The norse gods own the days of the week.

Sunday is the day for the sun.
Monday is for the moon.
Tuesday is Tyr's day. He is not as well known as Oden, Thor or Loki...but was important enough to get a day of the week. God of War God of Judgment...Look him up and never look at Tuesday the same again.
Wednesday is Woden (or Odin as you know him: Thor's dad).
Thursday is Thor's day
Friday is Freya day.
And Saturday is Saturn's (zeus's dad) day—that Roman influence back in again.

And that is how the old gods still serve us.

Remember you are an animal

A large portion of the populace will say "I am not an animal. I am a human". This is an incorrect assumption that being human somehow makes us not animals.

You should always keep in mind that although, as a human, you have so many requirements, and you might seem more busy than what you deem an animal, you still have all the base needs of an animal, and you are driven primarily by them instead of your intellect.

Food
Shelter
Sex
And in the case of primates and other highly intelligent species (Dolphins ...Killer Whales) Socialization

Keeping this in mind will also make you more aware of your limitations. When wondering why humans cannot do something, look to our closest animal ancestors—the primates.

Primates suffer from the awareness and separateness of a better intellect than most animals.

They have problems like.
InFighting
Family Problems
Depression

And they are exceedingly clever and resilient.

Yet they keep helping each other...and that is how they move forward.

Respect your Elders

It is amazing how much you can learn from people who are older than you.
So this applies not just to your parents and family who raised you but ALL people older than you.

And this applies to all stages of life.
It is not like you ever stop learning.

They can be work mentors; They can be friends of a friend…
If they have even 10 years over you they have more life experience. If they tell you something, at least listen.

Your Star

Is it daytime?
Look up in the sky. Do you see the sun? It is all ours, as far as we know.

At this point of writing in 2020, there is no KNOWN intelligent life within our solar system.

The sun provides everything: The coal and natural gas you burn for heat and energy. It's sunlight from your star, trapped by plants long since dead.

If you give thanks to anything but your elders, give thanks to your star.

Prayers versus Hope

When I decided to not be a catholic any longer, I decided not to believe in prayers anymore. But I did not stop believing in hope.

Hoping for something and praying for something are very similar. You do want the best outcome to occur, but asking someone specific *might* make you feel better.

But actually believing in the statistics of actual success is infectious and better for the whole group.

Never let hope die.

How you should treat other religions

With respect.
Always treat religion with respect, unless it is used as a weapon.

To be honest, the way you should treat other religious texts is like parables or stories meant to teach you a lesson. Do not treat them as past examples of events that occurred.

Tell me, do you treat the world like Thor and Odin crafted it? Or Zeus and Athena? Or any major deity of the past that is no longer worshipped?

We have no proof these moments occurred. And even if they did, the past has been edited to make it shinier.

Try to garner the lessons put down and edited, but try not to cling to it as a reality.

Humans are social beings

I think it was watching the film *Blackfish* that I really got how pretty much ALL intelligent mammals are social beings.

Like they NEED others of their kind.

Now, some of us might feel like we don't need people as much, because we find them tiresome as well. But if you ever find yourself low, and you can't figure out why, go visit some friends or acquaintances and talk about it. The whole process might make you feel better.

YOU NEED OTHER PEOPLE.

OTHER PEOPLE NEED YOU.

Likewise if you choose to ostracize someone family member or friend, you are hurting them more than you will ever realize. And unless it truly is unforgivable (they killed your father, they raped your mother), you and the party involved are better off moving to forgiveness and moving on with life.

The world is a sphere

It bothers me that flat earth has become a discussion point.
I feel people like this should not be allowed a cell phone.

I mean a cell phone relies on the fact that there are satellites orbiting the earth and towers to triangulate signals to make calls, which is all dependent on the fact that the earth is a sphere hurtling through space.

If they can't accept this concept, they SHOULD NOT BE ABLE to play with the toys.

Racism

Racism is the stupidest thing, maintained by parents teaching their children to be racist through their actions.

Keep in mind that racism is not about words at all but about how you treat other human beings. If you are white and privileged, you probably have done at least *some* slightly racist things without even being aware.

If you ever complimented an asian or indian person, on the phone or in person, on the execution of their English—that is SLIGHTLY racist.

If you can ask a friend who experiences this type of racism, then you will understand.

But there is a solution: keep making friends with tons of people of different cultures and races and whatever.

The more people you talk to and understand WE ALL WANT THE SAME SHIT, the more you will grow away from racism.

Racism is built into all the systems around us, and we must retrain our thinking to keep chipping away at it.

Neither you nor I will eradicate racism. But keep chipping away at it and it actually could fall away in future generations.

Remember, it's not the language, it is the actions and thoughts.
If you find yourself thinking, "But those people are…". That is racism.

"Those people are good at doing hair."
"Those people are good at cooking barbecue."

It doesn't matter if it is a compliment. Prevent yourself and others from putting a certain group into a subsection.

The Struggle

By now you should be aware that life is a struggle.
Life is more unfair and more of a struggle for some people versus others.
But we all struggle.

Pay attention to the little adjustments you and others around you make
to continue struggling, not just people close to you, but people in history
also.

There are many people who, when jailed wrongly, chose to focus inward
and focus on the small tasks to toughen their mental faculties, so they
would make it out the other side.

Some revel in the struggle they face. Some just take one moment and
one day at a time.

Whatever works, as long as you and others persist in the struggle. And
you keep moving forward.

The more you struggle, and the more you succeed in not being defeated
by what the world throws at you, the more you will be able to glance off
future events and keep moving forward.

The same way fighters toughen their hands and hide so the fight does
not sting them, you toughen your internal mental state to the point that
the worst can happen and you just say, "It's all part of the struggle," and
keep moving forward.

If a child or adult asks you point blank, do not lie. Do not say life is easy.
Tell them,
"Life is hard and unfair at times, but it is still a gift."
Use all your milliseconds.

Your mind can get into ruts like a road.

A road that is not paved can sometimes form a deep rut, because of a rainy season and cars.

I don't know if there is a term for the psychological equivalent, but your brain can also form these ruts.

If you are going through a tough period and your escape is fried chicken and ice cream, then it could always be these things going forward. Be careful with the habits you form.

And work on the bad habits you already formed.

Oh my God

In sudden awareness of a situation you might say.

Oh my God
Jesus christ
Or something else deity specific.

If you are trying to be deity free, try "gods". It specifies no alignment but still makes you relatable in the moment.

Gods, that was a good meal.
Gods, that was great sex.
Gods, you are the best thing I've found in this world.

Relationships are a very important job.

Earlier, I pointed out that we need people.
That being said; maintaining a group of people you value can sometimes be taxing. You may have to let people go at times. It requires maintenance on both sides.

This is true of relatives, spouses, and friends.

If there is a fight one of you has to try and repair it.
If it is always you who repair it, you should point this out to them.

If you keep reaching out to a friend or mentee that does not respond, let them go.

But try to be forgiving as much as possible.

Self-Betterment

There will be a certain time in your life where teachers, relatives, friends, and mentors are not really teaching you anything new related to your career or you.

I cannot predict when this time will come. For me, it really did not come until I got my true career rolling. It is at this point you need to learn to focus yourself on self-betterment.

Instead of others pointing you at things that could or would make you better, it is you who takes a hard look at yourself and decides that, because of certain flaws or lacks or holes in knowledge that, you research and find a path to educate or gain experience that will help you grow, either as a human or as a worker.

This is what self-betterment is and once you discover it you will always swing back to it and keep "filling out you."

Filling out you is the best thing you can do to attract more friends, more lovers, and more jobs. Now it does not have to be entirely skills. It can be attitude adjustments. It can be just a hobby that you want to be better at.

For example, say your work output is fantastic, but your stress management is horrible, and you constantly blow up at people you love and people you interact with. A self-betterment path might be simply investing in either therapy or therapeutic paths that teach you how to manage stress better so you never reach the point of blowing up.

Another example would be this: Say you enjoy doodling because it relaxes you but some people have commented that your doodles are fairly high quality but "not quite there". You could invest in art instruction or research and practice to improve your drawing skills.

I am sure if you think really hard in this area and make it a priority, you will discover other ideas than the couple I mentioned.

Now

This is something I struggle with, and my martial arts master says I will get better with age and practice.

But you should focus and live in the NOW. Not the future, and NEVER the past.

Thinking of these things is not necessarily bad, but your main focus should be the now.

Because that is where everything important happens.

You weren't born a certain amount of years ago in a certain spot. You were born in the NOW of that day time and spot. And the world reacted to you in real time.

You will not die in the future. When you die it will be the *now*.

Someone suggested an exercise to understand the now and why you should pay attention to it.

Close your eyes and clap your hands together
When did it happen? Now.
Will it ever happen again? No. Never again will it be that sharp and that echoey at the same time it was the now.

Pay attention to all the rich details of every moment in the now, and you will have a rich and rewarding life.

Stories

The story of how spiders came to be

This is a story that you can probably google up on the internet but I am placing it in this book from my memory of the story.

If I leave out any details it is simply because I did not want to crib from another writing of it. And it is a good story.

It is a story from Greek and Roman mythology

There was once a weaver named Arachne (you may notice this is the root of the word for fear of spiders and the study of them).
She was such a good weaver that the townspeople joked she was competition for the goddess Athena.

So Athena came down to earth disguised as an old woman and challenged the young lady to a weaving competition.
Arachne agreed and they were off weaving.

Athena honestly was having trouble keeping up with the fabulous Arachne.
And when she admitted her defeat, Arachne said, "Well you are just an old woman."

At this point Athena appeared as herself to the young woman and cursed her to weave forever and turned her into a spider.

What is the lesson of this story? Humility.

No matter who you interact with, be it a god or not, if you use haughtiness and pettiness you can leave these people or gods with a bad impression, and it could blow up in your face later. You could lose an opportunity like not getting a job you want. Or you could be turned into a spider.

The Beatitudes

Blessing from Jesus in the New Testament

These are copied from the wikipedia page on the subject.

> Blessed are the poor in spirit,
>   for theirs is the Kingdom of Heaven.
> Blessed are those who mourn,
>   for they will be comforted.
> Blessed are the meek,
>   for they will inherit the Earth.
> Blessed are those who hunger and thirst for righteousness,
>   for they will be filled.
> Blessed are the merciful,
>   for they will be shown mercy.
> Blessed are the pure in heart,
>   for they will see God.
> Blessed are the peacemakers,
>   for they will be called children of God.
> Blessed are those who are persecuted because of righteousness,
>   for theirs is the Kingdom of Heaven.
> Blessed are you when people insult you, persecute you and falsely say all kinds of evil
>   against you because of me.
> Rejoice and be glad, because great is your reward in heaven, for in the same way they
>   persecuted the prophets who were before you.

There are many themes within this text, and it does not hurt to read them and their interpretations.

David and Goliath

This is an old testament story that is not as big with Jews as it is with Christians.

But it is the story of a regular guy beating a giant, probably a huge imposing guy like Abraham Lincoln. And he beats him with a simple sling, a thing that throws a stone real fast.

Moral
Do not give up, even when the odds are against you.

The story of the teacher and her quarters

There one was a teacher in a very low-income school that had several shelters that fed many very impoverished students into its already low-income population. She enthusiastically collected state quarters, back when it was popular around 2006.

She went from classroom to classroom asking fellow teachers if she could come in and talk and display the three different beautiful coin "books" that colorfully showed all fifty states on a map and their individual US coins of 25 cents each. Each book probably worth about $13 plus the cost of the empty $10 booklets. All the fellow teachers warned her that the kids would probably take coins from the cardboards, ruin the booklets, and she would be better off not bringing in the collections.

But of course, the slight risk was well worth the learning and the experience. She passed the 3 books all around in many different classrooms, so children could touch and take coins out and put them back in. The lesson included the value of each coin, presidents, the particular pride that states maintained, and more.

When she got home, she went about cooking and tending to her family, then decided to check on just how many coins might be missing. She became almost smug about the fact that not one was gone and decided to only say so to the few teachers she considered true friends.

At school the next day, to her sometimes-teary surprise, kids came up to her all day with quarters in their hands saying, "Here,Mrs. L., can you put this in your collection, and I will look for more". For the next few days, she came equipped with 10 quarters that were not state quarters but the older ones with eagles, weighing down her pockets so that she could trade with those many generous kids. The trade was only for her own conscience, she already had 3 full sets of quarters for all 50 states and the additional territories. They valued her presentation far more than the chance for a bag of chips or freeze pops.

This is just one of many small but memorable touching events in the life of any one working with groups of children. Adults learn far more from working with children than they initially come to give.

Themes: try not to be judgemental, and people surprise you everyday.

Belling the Cat

This is from *Aesop's fables*; It's pretty cool.

Once upon a time, all the mice met to discuss their enemy, the cat. One mouse had a great idea.

"We just need to tie a bell around the cat and when the cat approaches it will ring and warn us."

And an older mouse said "That is a great idea, But who is brave enough to do it?"

And nobody volunteered.

Theme: Sometimes it is just a people problem, and people are extremely hard to deal with.

The Gift of the Magi

by O'Henry
(Note this is a public domain story but you can still purchase O'Henry stories and enjoy them)

Was never a fan of the title of this story because of the religious overtones but it is a great story nonetheless.

It is the story of a husband and wife. The wife has beautiful long hair. The husband has a classy, old, gold pocketwatch. Besides that they are close to poor but happy and in love.

Come Christmas time, each of them desires something that would enhance this one thing about the other. For the wife, it is these combs she has admired in a store forever. For the husband, it is a classy chain to hang his pocketwatch from.

Come Christmas day.
The wife has cut her hair and sold it for wigs to get cash to buy the chain for his pocketwatch.
When he comes home he gives her the combs he bought by selling the pocketwatch.

Theme: Love is NEVER completely understood, and that is why it is so beautiful.

Oh we are just going to wait

This is the story of a boy and his father.

One day when the father was going to cut wood in the forest. The boy went with him. The boy would walk around the forest while he waited, and usually afterward they would get ice cream at this cheap place on the way home.

While in the forest, the boy heard his father calling him. When he arrived there was a big gash in his father's leg, and his father said, "We'll have to go".

When they got back to the city the father pulled over to the ice cream place.
And the boy was like, "But Dad, your leg…"
And the father said…"Oh we will get there and just WAIT"

So they got ice cream.
And sure enough, the father was right. Despite having a bleeding gash in his thigh they both waited a LONG TIME for stitches.

Lesson: Always listen to those with more life experience than you.

Suck It Up

So my mom was a fan of the phrase, "Suck it up."

Having the internet, I one day found where this phrase came from.

Supposedly from pilots (not sure if it was WW1 or WW2) where wearing a mask was the norm.

But if you puked in your mask, the best thing to do was to "suck it up". It was gross but you would asphyxiate if you did not.

When I told to this to my mother, she was older (maybe a grandma)
And she said "Gross, I wish I'd never used that phrase"

And I said, "I like the phrase much better now"

Theme: Sometimes the hardest path is the correct one.

Story of Attitudes

This is a made-up story that expresses a concept that a person who is my senior conveyed to me one day.

Once upon a time, two friends went to a housewarming party. Now it was a really nice house, and they knew the people really well, and they were having a good time.

At some point the host (the owners of the house) came out with champagne. Now, the first person almost dropped the champagne but recovered and didn't drop it. The second person also almost dropped the champagne but did not and recovered it.

The first person was in anxiety for the rest of the party because they remember they almost dropped the champagne on the beautiful new carpet. The second person moved on and said "But, I didn't drop it". They totally moved on, had conversations with the people there and enjoyed themselves.

The theme here is to not to be constantly caught up with your past and instead to live in the now because timewise, there is only the now.

The best fire I ever lit

So as a teenager, I found certain chores not as bad once you learn the Rhythm.

One of these chores was lighting the wood stove when I would get home (because I would get home first).

As time went on I got better at this skill and I got the Rhythm. "Let it have a little air, let it have a little fuel, and it's a little here, until it gets good."

And then one day I got it going really, really good and swung my head and checked on the wood stove and the door was glowing red. My father checked on it a little later and yelled at me for getting it going so hot.

But to this day, I feel nothing but pride in lighting a fire that was the level that was necessary to possibly make iron or other metals back before there were factories.

Opinions

Now that I got your ear

I will not bullshit you if you have read this far—you buy into some of *my* bullshit.

I am not afraid now to let loose with opinion.

Let us be clear on the distinction between opinion and fact. Opinion always exists in someone else's head. Fact exists because everyone can measure something that is real.

We all have our personal level of bullshit, and we share some of those concepts.

It is not a bad idea because life experiences bring us together.

Here are some *opinions*.

The two tasks of Life

Life can be separated into two Tasks:

1. Chores/Work
2. Building Memories

So most of the day-to-day of life is taken up by Task #1, which means doing stuff to earn money and doing stuff to keep your life afloat. It is up to YOU to make sure you execute #2.

You have to make plans and let go of TASK #1 to occur.

Go out and build memories NOW. It is really what makes you want to KEEP LIVING.
And that is my opinion.

You are never really alone

Think about it you have had times where you felt so alone because you did not visit friends or have a wife or husband or girlfriend or boyfriend.

But you were *not*.

There was the mailperson, bringing you mail.
There was the gas person, reading your meter so you have heat.
There was the store clerk, ringing up your groceries.

We are so continuously dependent on other people, we sometimes do not see them all.

So the next time you feel alone, *look harder*.

Arguments

No matter what you think, it takes more than one person to argue.

You might be convinced that the other person is completely WRONG.
But if you get into an argument, it involves both of you. Both of you are at fault for having an argument.

I wrote this section after having an argument with someone I cared about who completely was convinced it was *all my fault*.

And I thought "No, that logic is bullshit."

But I hate myself so much I believed it anyway.

Focus on making Friends Always

So this is something I have learned.
I made friends and know outgoing people.

I am *not* outgoing. But I see outgoing people how they make friends in checkout lines, in traffic, and waiting for the bus. And they learn something about people and themselves by doing this constantly.

So I do this, and I suggest you do too.
The next time you hear one of these people say something interesting, try talking to them.
It will not hurt you and you can back away or go somewhere else if it becomes too difficult.

But learning about others is *never* a waste. And if you make friends with random people random people might stand up for you. "What about this nice person (that is you)? They have been waiting in line forever."

When others are sexually attracted to you

To be honest, whatever form this interest takes, you should take it as a compliment that you put yourself together enough in this world that someone finds you a *find*.

Even if it is just physical and they do NOT understand or see you, at least you are physically attractive to that person.

There will be days that you don't feel that you are ever or ever will be.

It is always a compliment, even if you don't swing that way.

Do not let your limitations define you

So we all have limitations. For me, I have trouble talking to people.

So this is what I mean instead of defaulting to that trouble, I choose occasionally to rise above it to experience life, when I am in line in a supermarket, and I find a person interesting.

Like if you have a fear of heights I think you should try to beat it you should either seek therapy or or try to beat it yourself.

The point is this: we all have limitations. Do not think you are subpar to others, because you always lean into them.

"Oh, don't ask them. They are afraid of spiders and will stop working digging the ditch."

"Oh, don't ask them. They are afraid of sweating in outdoor labor."

Know your limitations. Rise above them and only the closest to you can know.

Listen to the ticking

I am of the belief that, based on a bunch of varied things that affect you, you are granted a lifespan of so many milliseconds.

Now, lots of things come into play. Your biology inherited from your family.Your upbringing and environment.

And then as you live, you slowly whittle your life away with vices and drama. And then you are gone.

And once you realize this you can start to hear the clock ticking every day when you wake up.

And you think "What have I done today?" And you will find your drive.

That is what I think.

Everyone is an asshole

See when I was young I made some wisecracks that my parents said "You asshole."
And I knew I was in...the whole trick is to advance to the adult world.

But they knew they couldn't say it in public....so they shortened it to "AH."

And one year (I think for Halloween with the relatives) they put it on a card (gods i wish i had kept that card). But they got lears from relatives and they stopped doing it.

And they stopped doing it.

They started referring to me as "little man". Which was not as fun.

And this is why I was disappointed: see everyone is an asshole. But so few males are actually men.

Theme: Keep yourself humble. You are still a fool, still an asshole. But then, everyone is...

Telling Stories

Part of what I find about telling stories is not just telling them to groups but actually writing them down, so you can see the words and actually make the words better.

Make the story have an arc and some punch. Writing it down lets you focus on the affectations of your voice and expressions on your face when telling stories.

The main thing is keep telling the same stories in different crowds, and try editing them and rewriting them when you have down time.